Phases

Maria Weissman

Phases

To all those who have gifted me with their love.

Thank you.

I.   YOU

you taught me to waltz but wouldn't feed me

to run but wouldn't nurture me

I know how to whip my body
into a frenzy of torturous determination
but sustenance eludes me, still

your main gift was unintentional clarity

always teaching me
no matter how much
I beat my body into submission
your love would never be found

you can't force something from nothing
no matter how fast you go

II.   1/2

I get now why time forces us
to move so cruelly forward,
the endless march on

I'd give up my future
to live in a memory loop with you,
back then

I try to collect our memories now
like postcards
I never wanted any from that time before

but now you're gone and it's all I have

sure the world around us was torturous
but I had you then, at least

not now

there's such a void
and it'll never be filled

and it's not ok

we were supposed to have
our future

they robbed us of our innocence
but the future was supposed
to be ours, together

instead it's rubble
whispered ruins of what could've been

half-ghosts and half-memories

instead I'm here alone
the sole truth-teller in a sea of lies

I'd prefer madness

III.   KEEP GOING

did you know
no matter how many tears you cry
you still don't get swept out to sea?

somehow
you still don't drown in them?

I miss you so much

I didn't know
I could be in this much pain
and still exist

it seems like at a certain point
you should just disintegrate
and become part of the stars

but, no

you just keep going

IV.   ~~MAGIC~~

oh darling
the most interesting thing about you
was my love for you

how it made your eyes glow bright,
your face as luminous and haunting as the moon;
it never left my mind

how I longed to run my fingers through your hair
and never stop embracing
your body, hand-carved by God herself

but this type of love can't be sustained
on one side only
and the magic inevitably dried up, revealing to my
dismay and relief

that your eyes are simply windows into a soul
that doesn't love itself enough to love me properly

that your face is just a face
your hair just hair
and your body just a body

the most interesting thing about you
was my love for you
and without that,
your magic has all but disappeared

V. @NARCISSUS

I
am
not
a
plot
device
to
move
your
life
forward

//

why'd
you
get
me

to fall
so hard

just
to dispose
of me?

//

did I upset
you
because
you cared
about me
so deeply

or because
I beat you
at your
own game?

VI. GLORIOUS

I love you
and I haven't known
what to do with that

because what started so gloriously sunny
has become excruciating

what once felt so safe
keeps cyclically scorching me

I know
your actions have nothing to do
with me
(which isn't fair to me)

I know
your actions have everything to do
with them
(which wasn't fair to you)

and I know

I can't live in this cycle

so I must let you go,
softly, gently,
before all of our memories
go up in flames

I love you
and I now know what to do with that

goodbye

VII. MAGIC

we were a painful, ticking time bomb
due to fail from the start

still, I'm glad we started

I miss you

I cried after we first hung out
because I wanted you so much
but felt I wasn't right for you

and I wasn't

still, I'm glad we tried

your love was a soothing balm
rescuing my lonely soul

but as time marched on,
you couldn't stop yourself
from adding salt to my wounds

and that soothing healing
turned to raw, unending pain

anguish brings out the worst in people

but for a brief moment in time,
we were our best selves with each other

and it was magic

beautiful, unsustainable, heart-wrenching

MAGIC

VIII.   ME

I'd rather be alone
than squeeze myself into your world
to make us work

like a mermaid
who has unwittingly spent her life on land,
I've discovered where I belong
and it's not tap-dancing on shore for your affection

my magic is not on retainer
for whenever you feel like using such a creature

you're welcome to swim to me
but you'll likely be disappointed to discover
my magic runs out if I'm not cherished properly

that captivating mermaid turns into a slippery fish
that you can no longer get a hold of

P O O F

she's gone

MARIA WEISSMAN

is a musician and writer who

lives in Los Angeles, CA

@mariaweissman   mariaweissman.com

PHOTO CREDITS

Cover: (background) Igor Link

(moon) Mark Tegethoff

Back Cover: (author) Dominic Martinez

(background) Samuel Devantier